THATCH

THATCH

FEATURING

POLITICALLY CORRECT

~~MAN~~ **PERSON**

by *Jeff Shesol*

Vintage Books   A Division of Random House, Inc.   New York

A Vintage Original, April 1991
First Edition

Library of Congress Cataloging-in-Publication Data
Shesol, Jeff.
        Thatch — featuring P.C. person/by Jeff Shesol. — 1st ed.
            p.   cm.
        "A Vintage original" — T. p. verso.
        ISBN 0-679-73610-7
        I. Title.
    PN6727.S515T43   1991
    741.5'973 — dc20   90-51019
                                    CIP

Manufactured in the United States of America
10   9   8   7   6   5   4   3   2   1

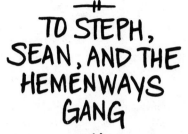

SOMEWHERE IN THIS GREAT LAND OF OURS...

...STANDS A GREAT UNI-VERSITY. A PLACE WHERE STUDENTS ARE DEVOTED TO THE PERFECTION OF BODY AND MIND...

... WHERE THE HALLS RESONATE WITH VOICES EAGER WITH CURIOSITY AND WISE WITH INSIGHT.

THESE GUYS DIDN'T GET IN.

TRIPP -- SETTLE THIS... WHO'S BETTER LOOKING -- SIMON OR GARFUNKEL?

PIPE DOWN! "SANFORD & SON"'S ON, MAN!...

CAST OF CHARACTERS, CONT'D.

SUMNER PHILLIPS, III

PREP-SCHOOLER-TURNED-DEADHEAD. FOLLOWED THE GRATEFUL DEAD LAST SUMMER. IN DADDY'S BMW.

I WANNA DANCE WITH SOMEBODY WHO LOVES ME...

PROF. ERIC WOODMAN

"WOODIE" TEACHES MODERN AMERICAN CULTURAL HISTORY. WOODIE DOESN'T BELIEVE IN EXAMS, QUIZZES, OR GRADES. WOODIE IS VERY POPULAR.

CLASS, WHO CAN TELL ME WHEN BOB DYLAN "WENT ELECTRIC"?

CHECK THIS OUT IN THE NEW "J. CREW" CATALOGUE!

POLKA-DOTTED P.J.'S. JUST CUDDLY.

NO, NO... **THIS!** "J. CREW PERSONALITY KIT: YOU'VE BOUGHT THE CLOTHES, NOW BUY THE MINDSET!"

LOOK -- IT COMES IN "OLD EASTERN WEALTH," "NEO-POST-YUPPIE," AND "SAILING TEAM CAPTAIN"! I'M CALLIN'!

THIS IS HOW THE "MOONIES" GOT OFF THE GROUND.

MY SAVINGS ACCOUNT NUMBER? HANG ON -- LET ME GET IT...

NICE SWEATER, "TRIPPY." WHERE'S SKIPPY, MUFFY AND THE GANG?

I KNEW YOU WOULDN'T AP-PROVE OF THE NEW ME.

BUT **SLOANE WHARTON** WILL APPROVE! WHEN SHE SEES ME IN THESE CLOTHES, SHE'LL GO WILD FOR ME!

OH -- SO **THAT'S** IT! TRIPP, THAT IS SO REPULSIVELY SHALLOW -- PLASTIC -- SUPERFICIAL ...

THEN AGAIN, SO IS SLOANE.

THE MAN'S A GENIUS!

HEY! MY "NEO-POST-YUPPIE" KIT HAS ARRIVED!

WHAT A QUALITY PACKAGE! FAKE BMW KEYS, POLO COLOGNE, A LIST OF WITTY THINGS TO SAY ABOUT BOOKS I'VE NEVER READ...

WAIT A MINUTE!

THIS IS NO "PERSONALITY KIT" -- IT'S JUST A COLLECTION OF PROPS... SUPERFICIAL IMAGE-MAKERS! WHAT A SICK DISPLAY OF MATERIALISTIC NARCISSISM!...

MY GOD... THE '80s ARE STILL WITH US!

WELL, THEY'D DAMN WELL BETTER BE... I PAID 75 BUCKS FOR THIS STUFF!

HMM... LOOKS LIKE S&L'S ARE UP, LBO'S ARE DOWN, AND THE FED'S RECONFIGURATING THE CONFIGURATIONS OF THE FIGURES AGAIN...

S&L'S ARE "UP"?

YOU'RE READING THE "WALL STREET JOURNAL"?

YOU GOT IT! AS MY PERSONALITY KIT SAYS, THE "JOURNAL" IS A HABIT WE NEO-POST-YUPSTERS CAN'T BREAK!

HMM...

FLIP FLIP

SOMEONE MUSTA TOOK THE DAMN COMIC SECTION!

HOW DO I BREAK THIS TO HIM?

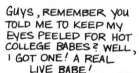

...YEAH, MOM. THE KID'S BEEN GREAT. WE'VE SEEN LECTURES, MUSEUMS... THE WORKS! SURE, YOU CAN TALK TO HIM.

MOM! THANKS FOR SENDING ME HERE! WE'RE TALKIN' BEER, BABES, A LITTLE '60s RADICALISM AND FREE LOVE... BOY, THESE GUYS ARE **OUT OF CONTROL**!

MMM HMM...

MOM SAYS YOU'RE GROUNDED.

SHESOL

HAVE YOU HEARD ABOUT THE GREENHOUSE EFFECT? AEROSOL IS DEPLETING THE OZONE LAYER -- IT'S GONNA KICK THE TEMPERATURE UP A FEW DEGREES.

INCREASE THE TEMPERATURE, YOU SAY?

YEP. GLOBAL WARMING.

FSSSSSST...

FRED'S RIGHT. THE 1970s ARE KAPUT. DEAD AND GONE. HISTORY.

I'VE GOTTA STOP LOOKING FOR ANSWERS IN THE PAST -- GOTTA TURN AROUND, FACE THE FUTURE!

SO I'M JUNKING ALL MY '70s PARAPHERNALIA -- THE GOLD MEDALLIONS, THE POLYESTER LEISURE SUIT, THE CHEST HAIR TONIC...

AND YOUR MONTE CARLO?

STRANDED IN THE MILE-LONG LINE AT THE GAS STATION.

I'VE FOUND IT, THATCH -- MY TRUE CALLING!

I'VE DECIDED TO ANSWER THE ART DEPARTMENT'S WANT AD FOR NUDE MODELS! WHAT A GREAT CHANCE FOR ME TO JOIN IN AN AESTHETIC EXPERIENCE WITH MY FELLOW ARTISTS!

WANTED

BIG BILL THE BARD MUST'VE BEEN THINKING OF ME IN THE BUFF WHEN HE WROTE, "WHAT A PIECE OF WORK IS MAN"!

YOU'RE A MAN OF LOFTY IDEALS, TRIPP.

PLUS, IT'S A SURE-FIRE WAY TO GET THE CHICKS.

Résumé

Résumé
J. Thatcher

Résumé
J. Thatcher

Résumé
J. Thatcher#!k@sjti

THIS, OF COURSE, NEVER HAPPENED TO LEE IACOCCA.

WOW! WHAT AN INCREDIBLE RÉSUMÉ! I NEVER KNEW YOU BUILT HOUSING FOR THE HOMELESS AND ADVISED CONGRESS ON EDUCATION POLICY!

HEH HEH

HEH HEH... THAT'S JUST A JOKE RÉSUMÉ -- I DIDN'T REALLY DO THAT STUFF. HERE'S MY REAL ONE...

IF YOU'RE GOING STRICTLY FOR LAUGHS, I'D GO WITH THIS ONE.

GIVE ME THAT!

HOWDY, WOMYN, MEN AND OTHERS... P.C. PERSON HERE, WITH A SPECIAL TREAT FOR YOU TODAY!
PC

IT'S MY NEWEST BOOK-O'-DOGMA: "HOW TO ARGUE THE P.C. WAY." IT'S REALLY QUITE SIMPLE, AS --
NO, IT'S NOT.
HOW TO ARGUE THE PC WAY

Reporter's Notebook
J. Thatcher

ASSIGNMENT:
Tripp Biscuit /
Womyn's Collective

Overcoming T. Biscuit's stubborn sexism is truly a considerable task — one that is, perhaps, insurmountable to mere mortals.

...KEEP ABORTION LEGAL... E.R.A. NOW... COMPARABLE WORTH... KEEP ABORTION LEGAL...

The womyn, however, appear to be making some progress.

COME ON, BUDDY... SNAP OUT OF IT!

OUR BODIES OUR SEL

- SIGH -
IT'S NO USE. HE'S ONE OF -- **THEM** NOW... THE POLITICALLY CORRECT.

DON'T LOSE HOPE, THATCH. I THINK HE CAN BE DE-PROGRAMMED.

YOU'RE NOT SUGGESTING --

YES. WE HAVE NO-WHERE ELSE TO TURN.

YA WANT US TO **WHAT?**

WAYLAND RUGBY

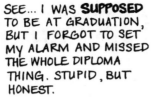

GLORY BE! SALVATION!

IS THIS YOUR MAIL-ORDER DIPLOMA?

YEP! "DIPLOMAS INC: SERVING YOUR DEGREE NEEDS, FASTER."

WAIT... WHAT'S THIS OTHER STUFF?... AN M.D.? A Ph.D.?

KIND OF LIKE BASEBALL CARDS, TRIPP? YOU KNOW, "COLLECT 'EM ALL"?

THEY WERE CHEAPER AS A SET, OK?

IT'S ALL OVER FOR ME... I'VE BEEN CALLED TO THE DEAN'S OFFICE. IF I'M LUCKY, THEY'LL JUST PADDLE ME.

COME IN, MR. BISCUIT.

TRIPP, WHAT'S THIS NONSENSE ABOUT YOU LACKING A HIGH SCHOOL DIPLOMA?

WELL, SIR, I'VE GOT THIS...

DIPLOMAS, INC.? MY ALMA MATER!

DUDE!

ALWAYS GOOD TO MEET A FELLOW-- WHAT IS OUR MASCOT, ANYWAY?

DON'T BELIEVE ONE WAS LISTED IN THE CATALOGUE, SIR.

THATCH?! IS THAT YOU?

SURE IS, MAN!

I THOUGHT YOU GOT A MEDICAL EXEMPTION!

I DID. BUT I COULDN'T LET MY BUDDIES GO IT ALONE... I'M HERE AS A REPORTER!

THAT'S HOW I CAN DO MY DUTY TO MY COUNTRY -- FOLLOW YOU GUYS ON A MISSION, AND SHOW THE FOLKS AT HOME WHAT IT MEANS TO BE AT WAR! I'LL LIVE, BREATHE THE SOLDIER'S LIFE!

WHERE'S YOUR GEAR?

GEAR? I'VE GOT AN AIR-CONDITIONED SUITE AT THE SAUDI HILTON!

NEW DRAFTEES. BLACK, WHITE, RICH, POOR... THIS DRAFT GETS 'EM ALL.

POOR KIDS.

SCARED STIFF -- EVERY ONE OF 'EM.

YEP. FEAR -- THE GREAT EQUALIZER.

SOUNDS LIKE ONE'S PUTTING UP A FIGHT...

THERE'S ONE IN EVERY GROUP. ONE THAT'S GOTTA BE DIFFERENT. THEY'LL BREAK 'IM...

ALL RIGHT, "CORPORAL KLINGER"... OFF WITH THE GODDAMN CAPE...

I, SIR, MOST CONSCIENTIOUSLY OBJECT.

TERRIBLE. IF I KEEP THIS UP, I'M GONNA BE PAINTING CLOWNS FOR SHOPPING MALL ART VENDORS.

I'VE BEEN TOO DAMN HAPPY LATELY... SUFFERING IS THE KEY TO CREATIVITY, YOU KNOW.

WHAT?

I MEAN, LOOK AT ANDY WARHOL... JACKSON POLLOCK...

GREAT. TWO GUYS WHO LED MISERABLE LIVES...

... UNTIL THEY DIED, BITTER, DESPONDENT AND ALONE.

NOW IF I COULD ONLY TAP INTO THAT WITHOUT RUINING MY WEEKEND!..

WHERE'S TRIPP?

OH, HE'S OUT SUFFERING.

SUFFERING?

HE THINKS HE MUST TRULY SUFFER TO GROW AS AN ARTIST.

GOSH... I JUST HOPE HE DOESN'T DO ANYTHING TOO... DRASTIC...

AAAAHHHH!...

NEW KIDS ON THE BLOCK

THE GREAT COLLEGE SCANDALS, IT SEEMS, ARE ALL IN THE PAST.

- HERALD -
IVY LEAGUE CRACK DEAL

POST 15¢
HOOKERS

- INDEPENDENT -
STUDENTS DEMAND SUICIDE PILLS

- TIMES -
STAR PLAYER CAN'T READ
"TOO BUSY" SAYS GUARD

WAYLAND UNIVERSITY HAD MORE THAN ITS SHARE OF THE GLORY, THE PRESTIGE, THE MEDIA ATTENTION...

NEWS 4

BUT ITS DAYS AS A PRESS DARLING HAVE LONG PASSED. THUS, THE ADMINISTRATION HAS DECIDED TO CONVENE...

SCRIBBLE SCRABBLE

...THE UNIVERSITY SCANDAL COMMITTEE.

CELEBRITY DAUGHTER JUNKIES.

TOO '80s.

TO GET WAYLAND BACK IN THE PAPERS, WE NEED TO GET STUDENTS RILED UP. IF WE DEPRIVE THEM OF SOMETHING THEY TAKE FOR GRANTED...

FREE SPEECH! THAT CAUSED QUITE A STIR AT BERKELEY IN THE '60s...

NO... SOMETHING SIMPLER... NEW...

TOMATOES!

WHAT?!

STUDENTS'LL RALLY FOR TOMATOES?

ARE YOU KIDDING? IT TOOK RIOT POLICE TO QUELL LAST YEAR'S PROTEST OF THE CHICKEN CUTLET SHORTAGE!

THANKS FOR COMING, BISCUIT. I HOPE WE'LL GET A CHANCE TO WORK TOGETHER.

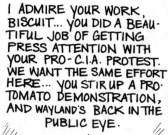

I ADMIRE YOUR WORK, BISCUIT... YOU DID A BEAUTIFUL JOB OF GETTING PRESS ATTENTION WITH YOUR PRO-C.I.A. PROTEST. WE WANT THE SAME EFFORT HERE... YOU STIR UP A PRO-TOMATO DEMONSTRATION, AND WAYLAND'S BACK IN THE PUBLIC EYE.

IT'S A PERFECT CHANCE FOR YOU TO EARN THE GRATITUDE OF THE ADMINISTRATION, AND THE RESPECT OF YOUR PEERS...

WELL, I'D LOVE TO HELP, **BUT...**

... AND A GOOD CHANCE TO HAVE THAT "NAKED SERENADING" INCIDENT WIPED OFF YOUR RECORD.

THRILLED TO WORK WITH YA, BOSS!

YOU'RE REALLY **THAT** SERIOUS ABOUT THE TOMATO SHORTAGE?

YOU BET! AND I THINK A STUDENT COALITION IS THE WAY TO GO!

... AND, OF COURSE, THE FIRST STEP TO A SUCCESSFUL COALITION IS A QUALITY ACRONYM.

HMM... LET'S SEE...

ACTUALLY, I'VE ALREADY GOT AN IDEA... WHAT DO YOU THINK OF "TOMATO REVOLUTIONARIES + IRRITATED, PROTESTING PROLETARIANS"?

"TOMATO REV--"

I CAN HEAR THE CROWDS NOW... "T.R.I.P.P.! T.R.I.P.P.!..."

SHESOL

I DREAD SPRING WEEKEND. WILD DRUNKENNESS ISN'T REALLY MY SCENE.

AND THIS "ALTERNATE SPRING WEEKEND"? WHAT WEENIES. I HAVEN'T PLAYED "CAPTURE THE FLAG" SINCE 6TH GRADE P.E..

I KNOW... I'LL CREATE MY **OWN** KIND OF WEEKEND! REST, RELAXATION, AND CASUAL CONVERSATION WITH FRIENDS... IT'LL BE PERFECT!

JUST... **PERFECT.**

(GRUNT) DUDE... DID I MENTION WE'RE HAVING A LITTLE SOIRÉE TONIGHT?

Alternative ALTERNATIVE SPRING WEEKENDS

FIG. 1: EUROSOCIALITE.

THIS IS **SO** SLOW.

LET'S GO TO "THE CITY," SHALL WE?

FIG. 2: MACROBIOTIC.

SPRING! FLOWERS... TREES...

GRASS... WEED...

FIG. 3: FRESHMAN.

-GURP-

FIG. 4: LOSER.

OH YEAH?! AND WHAT'RE **YOU** DOING TONIGHT?

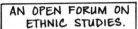

AN OPEN FORUM ON ETHNIC STUDIES.

SIR, I'M AWARE WE HAVE EAST ASIAN STUDIES, BUT WHY NO ASIAN-AMERICAN STUDIES DEPARTMENT?

YEAH!

HEAR HEAR!

YEAH! AND WHAT ABOUT BELGIAN-AMERICAN STUDIES?

AND **LITHUANIAN-UKRAINIAN**-AMERICAN STUDIES!

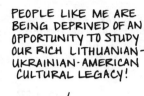

PEOPLE LIKE ME ARE BEING DEPRIVED OF AN OPPORTUNITY TO STUDY OUR RICH LITHUANIAN-UKRAINIAN-AMERICAN CULTURAL LEGACY!

UM... OUR STATISTICS SHOW EXACTLY **ONE** LITHUANIAN-UKRAINIAN-AMERICAN ENROLLED HERE.

WELL, IT'S HIGH TIME YOU START **RECRUITING** SOME!

...AND IF THIS UNIVERSITY DOESN'T INITIATE A FINNO-UGRIAN STUDIES PROGRAM, WE FINNO-UGRIANS ARE GONNA TAKE OUR FIGHT ALL THE WAY TO "DONAHUE"!

ETHNIC STUDIES NOW!

ER... MS. JOHANNSEN?

YES?

ETHNIC STUDIES NOW!

WE ADMINISTRATORS HAVE A LITTLE... **CONFESSION** TO MAKE...

YES?

WE DON'T EVEN KNOW WHAT A "FINNO-UGRIAN" **IS.**

A TYPICAL OPPRESSOR'S RESPONSE! DID YOU GUYS SEE HOW SHE JUST OPPRESSED ME?

AFTER THE HEATED ETHNIC STUDIES FORUM, A GROUP OF CONCERNED STUDENTS MEETS...

FIRST, WE SHOULD WRITE UP A LIST OF DEMANDS...

PUT ASIAN-AMERICAN STUDIES AT THE TOP OF THE LIST. AFTER ALL, WE **ARE** THE MOST OPPRESSED GROUP--

NO **WAY**, MAN!

WE ARAB-AMERICANS ARE **WAY** MORE OPPRESSED THAN YOU GUYS...

NO! WE ARE!

NO! IT'S US ARMENIANS!

ONE-UP-PERSON-SHIP IS AN UGLY SPECTACLE.

GIMME A BREAK! WE SERBS WERE GETTING STOMPED ON WHEN YOU ARABS WERE LIVING LIKE KINGS!...

A LIKELY SCENARIO.

THATCH, I FORGOT-- WHAT'S YOUR MAJOR?

"THATCH-AMERICAN STUDIES," OF COURSE-- AND YOU?

WHY, "KATE-AMERICAN STUDIES," OF COURSE. HOW 'BOUT YOU, REED?

MATH.

FASCIST.

About the Author

Jeff Shesol created THATCH during his senior year of high school in Colorado. He resurrected the character with the killer cowlick a year later at Brown University, where the strip appears in the Brown Daily Herald. THATCH is also carried by more than 200 other college newspapers, and has appeared in the pages of The New York Times, the Wall Street Journal, and Newsweek. After graduating in May 1991 with a B.A. in History, Shesol, a Rhodes Scholar, will head to Oxford University.